PEANUTS®

Doodle Book

■SCHOLASTIC

Produced under licence by
Scholastic Children's Books,
Euston House, 24 Eversholt Street,
London NW1 1DB, UK

Peanuts created by Charles M. Schulz
www.peanuts.com
© 2014 Peanuts Worldwide LLC

Internal designs produced for Scholastic by gas advertising

All rights reserved.
Published in the UK by Scholastic Ltd, 2014

ISBN 978 1407 15274 5

Printed in Italy

2 4 6 8 10 9 7 5 3 1

THIS BOOK BELONGS TO

_____

Charlie Brown

Loves

Snoopy, his beagle

Hates

The kite-eating tree

Crush

The little red-haired girl

Best friend

Linus

Sister

Sally

Charlie Brown fact

He manages the neighbourhood baseball team and he's always surprised when his team don't turn up in the rain.

I WONDER WHAT WOULD HAPPEN IF I WINKED AT THAT LITTLE RED-HAIRED GIRL...

NOTHING

© 1986 United Feature Syndicate, Inc.

PROBABLY BECAUSE SHE ISN'T HERE TODAY..

Snoopy

Loves

Linus's blanket

Hates

The Red Baron

Best friend

Woodstock

Sister

Belle

Brothers

Spike, Olaf, Marbles and Andy

Snoopy fact

His alter egos include Joe Cool, Flying Ace, Literary Ace, Legal Beagle and Beagle Scout.

IT'S GRATIFYING TO HAVE A DOG GREET YOU WHEN YOU GET HOME FROM SCHOOL..

10-23

SIGH

SCHULZ

Lucy Van Pelt

Loves

Being bossy

Hates

Being kissed by dogs

Crush

Schroeder

Brothers

Linus and Rerun

Lucy fact

Lucy always believes she is right and she even runs her own Psychiatric Booth.

Linus Van Pelt

Loves

His security blanket

Hates

Being called Sweet Babboo

Best friend

Charlie Brown

Sister

Lucy

Brother

Rerun

Linus fact

He believes that the Great Pumpkin will rise from the pumpkin patch on Halloween night.

COME WITHIN ONE FOOT OF THIS BLANKET, YOU STUPID DOG, AND YOU'LL REGRET IT FOR THE REST OF YOUR LIFE!

6-28

SCHULZ

CLOSE...TWELVE AND A HALF INCHES!

Peppermint Patty

Loves

Sports

Hates

D minuses

Crush

Charlie Brown

Best friend

Marcie

Classmates

Franklin and Marcie

Peppermint Patty fact

She likes to call Charlie Brown 'Chuck'.

THIS IS MY REPORT ON THE "KILLER BEES"

MANY PEOPLE ARE WORRIED ABOUT THE "KILLER BEES"

© 1986 United Feature Syndicate, Inc.

1-24

NOT ME

WHAT I WORRY ABOUT ARE THOSE "KILLER D-MINUSES"!

Marcie

Loves

School

Hates

All sporting activities

Crush

Charlie Brown

Best friend

Peppermint Patty

Classmates

Peppermint Patty
and Franklin

Marcie fact

Much to Peppermint Patty's
annoyance, Marcie insists on
calling her 'sir'.

I WAS ONLY TEASING YOU YESTERDAY, SIR.. CHARLES AND I WEREN'T REALLY TOGETHER...

YOU HAD ME PRETTY UPSET, MARCIE..

GETTING UPSET IS GOOD FOR YOU, SIR.. IT PREPARES YOU FOR ALL THE THINGS THAT ARE GOING TO HAPPEN TO YOU LATER IN LIFE...

6-23

YOU'RE A JOY TO BE WITH, MARCIE

Sally Brown

Loves
Getting her 'fair' share

Hates
Schoolteachers

Crush
Linus, her Sweet Babboo

Brother
Charlie Brown

Sally fact
She often gets her words slightly mixed up, much to everyone's confusion.

TELL MY SWEET BABBOO I'VE BROUGHT HIM A VALENTINE...

TELL HER I'M NOT HER SWEET BABBOO!

WHAT DOES HE KNOW?

Schroeder

Loves

Beethoven

Hates

Being interrupted while practising the piano

Schroeder fact

He insists that Beethoven's birthday should become a national holiday.

TOMORROW IS BEETHOVEN'S BIRTHDAY

SOME OF THE GREATEST MUSIC IN ALL THE WORLD WAS WRITTEN BY BEETHOVEN!

© 1980 United Feature Syndicate, Inc. 12-15

NO, HE WASN'T A BIRD!

Pigpen

Loves

Dirt

Hates

Being clean

Pigpen fact

He aspires to be class president one day.

"PIGPEN"! I HAVEN'T SEEN YOU FOR A LONG TIME...

OBVIOUSLY, YOU ARE JUST AS MESSY AS EVER!

THE WORLD NEEDS MESSY PEOPLE...

OTHERWISE THE NEAT PEOPLE WOULD TAKE OVER!

Franklin

Loves

His grandfather

Hates

Nothing

Classmates

Peppermint Patty and Marcie

Franklin fact

He sits one seat ahead of Peppermint Patty in class, which makes his school days unbearable.

MY GRAMPA HAD ANOTHER BIRTHDAY YESTERDAY..

8-14

© 1990 United Feature Syndicate, Inc.

HE SAID," I HAVE TO ADMIT THAT THE YEARS HAVE BEEN GOOD TO ME"

" BUT THE MONTHS AND WEEKS HAVE BEEN A LITTLE RUDE !"

Woodstock

Loves

Playing bridge

Hates

Being small

Best friend

Snoopy

Feathered friends

Conrad, Bill, Olivier, Harriet and Raymond

Woodstock fact

He speaks a language that only Snoopy can understand.

PSST! WAKE UP...IT'S ALMOST NOON...

Z

THE EARLY BIRD GETS THE WORM

© 1980 United Feature Syndicate, Inc.

THAT'S TRUE... YOU CAN GET PIZZA UNTIL MIDNIGHT!

Does Linus finally get to see the Great Pumpkin, or is it something else?

Fill the page with zig-zags to cheer up Charlie Brown.

Today, Franklin is pretending to be a sheriff.
Can you draw him a dusty old town to run?

Where's Joe Cool hanging out?

Snoopy's doghouse is a lot bigger on the inside than it appears. Can you decorate it for him?

What happens when the leaf lands on Snoopy?

Who's Charlie Brown giving a present to?

Snoopy's decorated his doghouse for American Independence Day on 4th July. Fill the sky with fireworks.

Woodstock is off on holiday but he needs some transport to get there. Can you help him out?

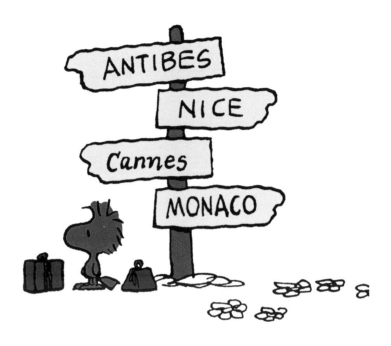

What does Snoopy do about Sally's lunch request?

Give Snoopy a pool to dive into.

Fill the page with Woodstock, Conrad, Bill, Olivier, Harriet, Raymond and all of their friends.

It can get a bit lonely in the desert for Snoopy's brother, Spike. Draw him some more cactus friends on the horizon.

Turn Flying Ace Snoopy's doghouse into a Sopwith Camel fighter plane, so he's ready to face his enemy, the Red Baron.

What's Woodstock flying over?

Help Snoopy and Linus build the tallest tower in the world.

Who's on the other end of the line?

What's caught Charlie Brown's attention?

Today, Snoopy is a world-famous pirate!
He and Woodstock are on the lookout,
but what have they spotted?

Who's Peppermint Patty passing the ball to?

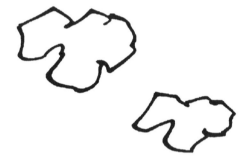

What danger lurks between Snoopy and Woodstock?

It looks like Charlie Brown doesn't want to be found.
What's he hiding from?

Quick! Someone's cleaned Pigpen up and he's not happy about it. Can you cover him in dust?

Does Snoopy behave or cause a disturbance?

Give everyone balloons!

Finish off Snoopy's look with a suitcase.
Don't forget to draw Woodstock on top of it!

Is grass really as good as snow to slide on? What happens next?

Woodstock and his friends are hanging out in this tree today but some of them are late.
Can you fit everyone in?

Snoopy is a master of disguise.
Give him some moustaches and wigs
so he can go about unnoticed.

What's Linus taking a photograph of?

Lucy is directing a play. Give her a cast to boss about.

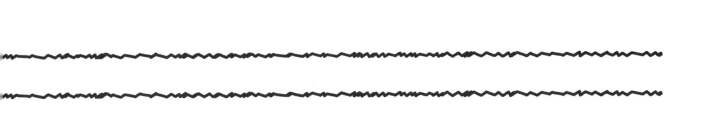

How does this raspberry-blowing match end?

Snoopy's wrapped up warm, but where is the snow?

Who is Charlie Brown playing Frisbee with?

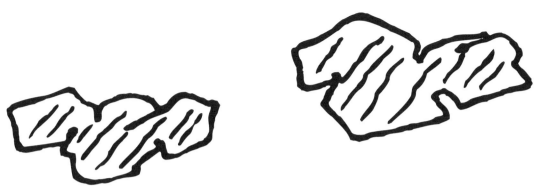

Lucy's wizard costume isn't quite finished. Can you finish her hat and add some accessories so she's ready to go?

Draw some authentic Western art for Spike's exhibition in the desert.

How does that beagle do it? Give Snoopy lots more Easter eggs from his admirers.

The world-famous detective, Snoopy, has discovered some interesting footprints. Can you draw a trail for him to follow?

What does Snoopy need to watch out for?

Draw the rest of the pumpkin patch for Sally and Linus to wait in for the Great Pumpkin.

What's Woodstock dreaming of?

What has Pigpen dug up? Is it something from an ancient civilization?

Charlie Brown doesn't have much luck flying kites. Draw him a new one that hopefully won't be destroyed by the kite-eating tree.

Decorate Snoopy's doghouse.

How do you think Peppermint Patty reacts to the first question of the year?

Give Snoopy and Woodstock some open road to ride along. Colour in the motorcycle, too.

Charlie Brown's been hard at work.
Draw the pile of leaves he's just raked up.

Snoopy's abandoned his aircraft, the Sopwith Camel, but where's he going to land?

Snoopy's rich! He's found the pot of gold at the end of the rainbow. But the rainbow needs a bit of work. Can you finish it off?

Where is Charlie Brown running off to with a love heart?

Linus's little brother, Rerun, needs some help creating bubbles, can you help him?

Finish off Snoopy's performance of 'Flashbeagle'.

Draw everyone queuing up for Lucy's psychiatric help!

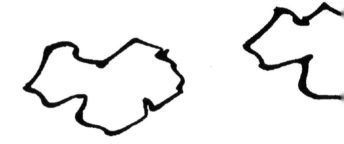

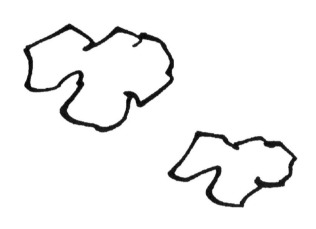

Add balloons, streamers, hats and anything else you can think of to get everyone in the party mood!

What else is Peppermint Patty still wearing from her ski trip?

What have Snoopy and Woodstock caught on their
fishing trip?

Add a sunset to make Spike's cactus orchestra even more impressive. Don't forget to add some musical notes, too.

Who's Peppermint Patty racing against on sports day?

What stops Charlie Brown from talking to the little red-haired girl?

What have Beagle Scout Snoopy and the scouts spotted at the top of the hill?

The Peanuts gang are showing off their dancing skills at a competition. Who do you think should get 1st, 2nd and 3rd prize? Give the winners some trophies.

Cover Snoopy and Woodstock in bandages so they can be world-famous mummies with Linus.

Rerun is on the back of his mum's bike, hoping he doesn't fall off! Can you design a super-safe bike for him?

Charlie Brown doesn't have much luck with kites. What happens when he holds Peppermint Patty's kite?

Snoopy's disguised as a scarecrow but he's only half done. Can you finish him off? Remember to add Woodstock, too.

Can you design Linus a new blanket?

Oh no! Snoopy, Sally and Linus are gathering speed. Draw a huge pile of cushions at the bottom of the hill to protect their crash landing.

Snoopy's just pulled up at a beautiful country house.
Can you draw the house of your dreams?

Snoopy's in space and he wants to go for a moon walk. Finish drawing the moon so he can explore. Don't forget to add Woodstock, too.

What's Snoopy having for dinner?

Oh no! What are the Peanuts gang running away from?

How does Woodstock's dive end?

What smoke signals is Scout Master Snoopy's
fire sending up?

What has Sally spotted in the water?

What has sent Sally and Linus flying?

Snoopy has gone for a nap. What is he resting on?

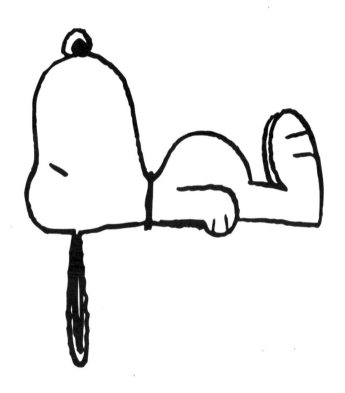

Everyone's enjoying a chat, but they haven't noticed the weather. What's it doing?

What has Lucy found in the sock?

Give Snoopy and Woodstock an umbrella to stop them getting even wetter.

Charlie Brown and Linus have collected lots of snow, but what are they going to build?

What has Rerun got in his wheelbarrow?

End Linus's waiting and draw the Great Pumpkin!

It's farewell from the Peanuts gang. Can you give them a banner to say 'goodbye' properly?

These two best friends are stargazing. Fill the
night sky with shooting stars.